The  Rough Guide to

50 Great UK
Events 2008

NEW YORK • LONDON • DELHI

www.roughguides.com

Publishing information and credits

Authors: Kieran Meeke and James Ellis,
with Zena Alkayat, Philip Blackmore, Marc Dodd, Graeme
Green, Fiona Macdonald, Paul Middleton, Chloe Scott, Lisa
Scott, Karen Stetch, Chris Stocks, Andrew Williams
Editor: Helena Smith
Design & layout: Diana Jarvis
Proofreader: Stewart Wild
Picture research: Lucy Schweitzer, Greg Meeson
Production: Vicky Baldwin
Project manager: Emma Traynor
Account managers: Dunstan Bentley (Rough Guides),
Fiona Allison (Metro)

Published 2007 by Rough Guides Ltd, 80 Strand, London
WC2R 0RL

© Rough Guides Ltd

Printed and bound by Butler and Tanner, UK

Image credits

Front cover Octopus kites © National Geographic Creative/Getty;
Back cover Hay on Wye Literature Festival © Andrew Fox/Alamy
p.6 Royal Ascot © Tim Graham Photo Library; **p.9** Hurdle Race,
Cheltenham Festival © Getty; **p.12** Modern Ballroom Competition © Geoff
A Howard/Alamy; **p.15** Antonio Maeso © Getty; **p.18** British Grand Prix at
Silverstone © Corbis; **p.21** Tiger Woods © AFP/Getty; **p.22** British National
Surfing Championships © PA photos; **p.25** Lin Dan at the All England
Open Badminton Championships © Lawrence Looi/Corbis; **p.26** Indoor
Windsurfing at the London Boat Show © Getty; **p.29** Erik Bloodaxe at
York Minster © Asadour Guzelian; **p.32** Medway Sweeps festival © Ian
Goodrick / Alamy; **p.37** World Bog Snorkelling Championship © PA Photos;
p.41 German marble player Andreas vom Rothenbarth © AFP/Getty;
p.43 Recieving Town Standard © South West Images Scotland/Alamy;
p.47 Seasick Steve at the Cambridge Folk Festival © Photo by Albanpix
Ltd/Rex Features; **p.50** Abergavenny Food Festival © Jeff Morgan food
and drink/Alamy; **p.53** BedZed © Open House London; **p.56** Market Hall
at the Abergavenny Food Festival © Jeff Morgan food and drink/Alamy;
p.59 Bulldog at Crufts International Dog Show © Corbis; **p.63** Henley Royal
Regatta © Getty; **p.64** Stella Artois Championships © Getty; **p.67** Royal
Ascot © Tim Graham; **p.69** Hampton Court Palace © Robert Harding; **p.73**
Braemar Highland Gathering © Getty; **p.74** Racegoer at Royal Ascot ©
Getty/Anwar Hussein; **p.76** Scottish sled dog rally © PA photos; **p.81** Royal
show at Stoneleigh © Royal Show; **p.84** International Balloon Fiesta ©
Getty; **p.89** Lewes Bonfire night © Getty/Dave Etheridge-Barnes; **p.90** The
Red Arrows © PA photos

Many of the images in this book have been taken with
cameras from the Canon EOS range.

For some events it is appropriate to check in advance
whether photography is permitted. If you plan to have your
pictures published then you need to gain permission from
any people you photograph. To cover all possibilities, it's
wise to ask your subjects to sign a model release form.

The **METRO** Rough Guide to

50 Great UK
Events 2008

CONTENTS

ICONIC 58

SPECTACLE 77

EVENTS BY MONTH 96

INTRODUCTION

Nowhere in Europe has the breadth of festivals and events that we have here in the British Isles. Inspired by this, the *Metro Rough Guide to 50 Great UK Events* describes the best, brightest and downright quirkiest events for 2008, aiming to give you a year to remember. We have split the book into five categories – Sports, Offbeat, Culture and Food, Iconic and Spectacle – so you can home in on your particular interests. At the end of each section we also give you a list of relevant **photography tips** that will ensure you end up with a great portfolio of images to remember each event by.

In our first category, **Sport**, as with the rest of this guide, we've tried to avoid the obvious. The Blackpool Dance Festival might not be top of everyone's list, but the resurgent interest in dance in our opinion makes it a sequinned stunner. Another criterion was beautiful and unusual settings, so the Isle Of Man TT roared into the final straight. In the **Offbeat** category, Arm Wars and the World Conker Championships are the last word in British eccentricity, while the Bog Snorkelling Championships offer a unique if bizarre location. Under **Culture and Food**, the Common Ridings in Scotland is a unique and colourful occasion with deep historical roots, while the bountiful produce of the Abergavenny Food Festival should provide plenty to attract wannabe gourmets. Our choices of **Iconic** events provide perfect opportunities for happy snapping – from the outrageous hats of Ascot to the graceful sails of Cowes Week. In the **Spectacle** category, too, photographers are spoilt for choice, from Chinese New Year in London, with its drummers and lion dancers, to the jousting knights of England's Medieval Festival in Sussex and the cross-country caper that is the Aviemore Sled Dog Rally.

Whether you bring your camera along or simply immerse yourself in the collective quirks, there's heaps to enjoy in the rich variety of events that Britain has to offer. Enjoy your 2008!

SPORTS

Cheltenham Festival

WHERE: Cheltenham Race Course, Gloucestershire
WHEN: March 11–14, 2008
WHY: The highlight of the National Hunt jump-racing season, Cheltenham may lack the mass appeal of the Grand National, but for sheer occasion and atmosphere it is unrivalled.
WHAT: For four days in mid-March Cheltenham is transformed as the racing community from around the world converge on the town. A fixture on the racing calendar since 1902, more than 230,000 people flock here each year and a phenomenal £500 million is bet on the 24 races during the week. With panoramic views of the surrounding Cotswold Hills, the course itself is set in spectacular surroundings.

The famous Cheltenham roar – the deafening noise the crowd makes as the horses battle it out down the long home straight – is one part of the experience. And the town itself comes alive as the hordes of visitors generate a great buzz and energy. The Festival is incredibly popular with Irish visitors, usually coinciding with St Patrick's Day (but not in 2008), and their presence adds another unique twist to the event. Run from Tuesday to Friday, the climax of the week is the Gold Cup, but other highlights include Tuesday's Champions Hurdle, Wednesday's Queen Mother Champion Chase and the World (Stayers) Hurdle on Thursday.

In terms of where you can watch the action there are a host of options, but Tattersalls (Tues–Thurs £35; Fri £50) on the south side of the course is one of the most popular and recommended enclosures. Admission to this part of the course also grants access to the Centaur – a new indoor arena with bookmakers, big screens and one thousand seats to watch the action. And while having a small flutter can enhance your excitement and enjoyment of the Festival, Cheltenham is an event which transcends not only betting but horse racing itself.

▶▶ www.cheltenham.co.uk

World Cross-Country Championships

WHERE: Holyrood Park, Edinburgh

WHEN: March 29–30, 2008

WHY: To watch the world's best distance runners warm-up for the Beijing Olympics in the picturesque surroundings of Holyrood Park.

WHAT: The world's toughest distance race has been held every year since 1973 and it returns to the UK after a nine-year absence when Edinburgh hosts the event. Big names expected to take part include Paula Radcliffe, who will use the race as preparation for an assault on the Olympic marathon title later in the year in Beijing, and rising male British distance star Mo Farah.

However, it is not just athletics on the agenda in the Scottish capital, with a host of events due to run alongside the feature races. They include parachute displays, school relay races, a mass five-kilometre road race and a "Kidzone" with an outdoor activity and adventure area. There's also a live concert on the Sunday afternoon after the closing ceremony which will feature some of the biggest bands across Scotland and the rest of the UK. Four main races take place on Sunday, with the men's (12km) and women's (8km) as well as their junior versions. Many of the world's top distance runners have won their first world titles in these junior races – including Radcliffe who triumphed in Boston, Massachusetts, back in 1992.

The centrepiece of the Holyrood Park course will be Haggis Knowe. This large rocky outcrop provides steep climbs and descents for the athletes as well as offering a superb vantage point from which you can view the entire course. Competition is always intense and the event has earned a reputation as the toughest to win in the athletics calendar. Unlike the Olympics where all the runners are separated into individual disciplines, this pitches all the world's top distance runners against one another. Holyrood Park promises to stage a memorable weekend and the fact that the venue is just a fifteen-minute walk from the centre of Edinburgh is a bonus. But best of all? It's free.

▶▶ www.edinburgh2008.org

First Test Match of the Summer at Lord's

WHERE: Lord's cricket ground, St John's Wood, London

WHEN: England v New Zealand May 15–19, 2008; England v South Africa July 10–14

WHY: Because however bad the national cricket team's form has been, the first Test of a series is always a time for renewed optimism. And if it's the first Test of the summer, well, even better.

WHAT: Some people think that a Test cricket match at The Oval is the one match to attend in an English summer. Traditionally the last game of a series, there's more often than not a lot riding on the game and as for The Oval itself – proud home to Surrey County Cricket Club and nestled just north of the Brixton badlands – well, it's the people's Test… innit?

But while The Oval may have the rowdy atmosphere, true lovers of the game know that if you only see one Test cricket match anywhere in the world, then it should be at Lord's.

The spiritual home of cricket is the bastion of the game, guardian of the rules, carer of The Ashes Urn and permanent residence of the game's former governing body the MCC (Marylebone Cricket Club). For a player, a Lord's Test is the pinnacle – so much so that to score a century here as a batsman or to take five wickets as a bowler sees the player's name immortalized on boards in the Pavilion's famous Long Room – more an art gallery than a member's area. And for the public the feeling of being steeped in the very history of leather-on-willow is very much the same – a feeling that probably leads to a more reverential atmosphere than at any other ground.

Test match series seem to come in bunches of three these days, so 2008 sees the Kiwis closely followed by the South Africans. Both promise to be excellent contests but even if they're washouts, there's still plenty to entertain here, whether you're taking in the amazing museum or simply people-watching.

▶▶ www.lords.org

Blackpool Dance Festivals

WHERE: Empress and Tower Ballrooms, Blackpool

WHEN: Junior Dance Festival March 24–30; Dance Festival May 22–30; Freestyle Championships October 11–12; Sequence Dance Festival October 18–21; National Dance Championships November 20–22

WHY: Because you may sit around glued to the telly watching the latest celeb dance-off on a Saturday night, but this is the real, sequinned, bequiffed and flared-trousered deal.

WHAT: The first years of the Blackpool Dance Festival in the early 1920s saw a host of novelty dances take to the floor and, alongside the more traditional waltzes and two-steps, country, stage and even Morris dancing all got their fifteen minutes of fame before being tapped on the shoulder and told to head back to the dressing room.

The competition may have taken a few years to, ahem, find its feet (it was even halted for two years from 1927–29 and again during the Second World War) but following the end of the war and the introduction of Latin American steps in the early 60s, the BDF has gone from strength to strength with ever more competitions added. Over recent years, aficionados have been able to sate their craving for choreography on an almost two-monthly basis, but there's no doubt which are the two most revered, and they both foxtrot onto the scene in spring.

First up in March is the slightly saccharine Junior Dance Festival which sees a host of Astaire and Rogers mini me's fight it out for titles in Latin, Ballroom and Sequence competitions. The only competition still held at the Tower Ballroom, the Junior Dance festival saw 2400 entries from more than thirty countries in 2007 but the figures are dwarfed by May's Blackpool Dance Festival. Now in its 83rd year and nine days long, there's ballroom, Latin, professional, amateur, dance team, team match and exhibition categories with some 3800 competitors from 62 countries taking part last year. Let's face the music, and dance…

▸▸ www.blackpooldancefestival.com

Isle of Man TT

WHERE: Isle of Man

WHEN: Provisional dates are May 24–June 6, 2008

WHY: One small island, public roads, twisting lanes and no speed limits. The Isle of Man TT is a race like no other.

WHAT: With no speed limits, the Isle of Man TT remains one of the fastest – and most dangerous – road races in the world. Since riders and their motorcycles first took to the twisting lanes and public roads of the almost 38-mile (60kms) circuit a hundred years ago, 224 competitors have died. Thousands flock to this Irish Sea island every year to watch and race in an event in which tragedy and triumph are so dramatically intertwined – while, on "Mad Sunday", members of the public can freely race the mountain section of the course.

Racing first started on the island in 1904 when a local law allowed roads to be closed for the Gordon Bennett car trials. On the mainland, speed limit laws stopped a British motorcycle race, so organizers hosted their event on the Isle of Man and the TT was born. The race quickly found fame across the world as racers such as Mike Hailwood, regarded by many as the greatest ever, thrilled the massive crowds. Legendary racer Joey Dunlop only cemented the TT's reputation. From his first appearance in 1976 to his last 24 years later, the Ulsterman racked up 26 TT wins and five F1 world titles. When he died racing in Estonia seven years ago more than fifty thousand fans attended his funeral.

The race has a new hero in the shape of John McGuinness, who, en-route to victory last summer clocked a first-ever 130mph lap on the Mountain course – although the event was again overshadowed by the death of one racer and two spectators. Despite this, the race goes from strength to strength, with the island transformed into a bikers' paradise for two weeks in May and June. This is road racing at its purest, an ultimate test of courage and skill.

▶▶ www.iomtt.com

Veuve Clicquot Gold Cup Polo Final

WHERE: Cowdray Park, West Sussex

WHEN: June/July, 2008. Final date to be confirmed

WHY: To see some of the finest horse-riders in the world play the sport of kings or, in the case of William and Harry, princes.

WHAT: Attracting the best polo players in the world, the Veuve Clicquot Gold Cup is a highlight of the summer, a day out in the sunshine to enjoy a glass of bubbly and rub shoulders with high society in a lovely setting.

Cowdray Park is the home of British Polo and some twenty thousand spectators will watch this tournament over three weeks. Polo is played by two teams of four and each game is divided into six "chukkers" of seven minutes each. Between chukkahs, spectators go onto the field to tramp in the divots thrown up by the horses. This is a chance to mingle on equal terms with everyone there – proof that polo, despite its reputation, has an egalitarian side. Back watching the game, you don't need to be a trained expert to understand the sheer skill involved in hitting a small ball with a long mallet from the back of a galloping horse. Most of the world's top players are Argentine, having been more or less born on the back of a horse, and their dashing Latino good looks are no doubt an important part of the sport's appeal for many.

Look closer, and you'll see that polo is pretty rough – in fact, a lot of the action takes place away from the ball. The rules strictly protect the horses, but rider-on-rider action is an essential element of the game. Keep your opponent away from the ball, and it's not going to matter how good he is at hitting it. Another key aspect of the game is celebrity-spotting. Helicopters and limos come and go regularly, disgorging or picking up millionaire team owners, pop and film stars and other famous faces. It all adds to the glamour and aura of an event that is guaranteed to fill the gossip columns for days afterwards.

▶▶ www.cowdraypolo.co.uk

Goodwood Festival of Speed

WHERE: Goodwood Park, Chichester, West Sussex
WHEN: July 4–6, 2008
WHY: It's a chance to see the finest cars and drivers of past years – and this year – in action in a beautiful parkland setting.
WHAT: From steam cars to today's F1 machines, Goodwood is a museum of cars in the round. Although the central event is a hill-climb, there's much more to Goodwood than that, with a 2.5km loose-surface rally track, design competition and a noted sale of cars and automobilia. The hill-climb is a two-kilometre-long stretch of road through the estate's parkland, where vintage cars, single-seaters, modern racing cars and motorcycles, among other categories, race against the clock. The rally course is always a popular event, too, also featuring cars from bygone ages – as well as the unveiling of the odd new-season car – with some famous names behind the wheel.

One of the things that makes Goodwood unique is the informal atmosphere, with a chance to rub shoulders with famous names, past and present, from John Surtees and Stirling Moss to Jensen Button and Fernando Alonso. The first Festival of Speed was in 1993 and it has grown year by year, with 250,000 visitors in 2007, while somehow still retaining the atmosphere of an exclusive private event. Part of its secret lies in the beautiful grounds that swallow up the spectators and cars, providing quieter corners for a picnic or a sudden glimpse of an iconic vehicle roaring past. And, of course, the sheer beauty of some of the cars on display is breathtaking, whether it's a gleaming vintage prewar Mercedes, or the latest sleek and threatening Formula One car.

For anyone who loves cars and motoring, this is a highlight of the year. More than two hundred trade stands provide everything you could wish for, from paintings to motorcycles, tools to workshop manuals. For those in the family less excited by cars, other diversions include live music and bravura air displays.

▶▶ www.goodwood.co.uk

British Grand Prix

WHERE: Silverstone Circuit, Northamptonshire

WHEN: July 11–13, 2008

WHY: Formula One is in vogue again thanks to the emergence of British sensation Lewis Hamilton and, with the race not guaranteed beyond 2009, there's no better time to go.

WHAT: Unlike the spectacular street circuit at the Monaco Grand Prix, Silverstone is unlikely to win any prizes for aesthetics, but this functional former air base in Northamptonshire comes alive once a year when the Formula One circus drives into town. Among the trailers of PRs, team mechanics and pit girls are some of the world's most fearless sportsmen, who will test themselves on one of the few seriously high-speed tracks in the world.

To add to the excitement, Britain now has a genuine star following the rapid rise of Lewis Hamilton. Like all major sporting events, the atmosphere and drama is ramped up to overdrive when a home favourite is thrown into the mix, and there's no doubt the Hamilton-factor will make the British Grand Prix one of the hottest sporting tickets of the year. Indeed, Silverstone has been home to several British successes in recent years, with David Coulthard the last to win in 2000.

It's hosted over three days, with practice on the Friday, qualifying (to determine the drivers' grid positions for the feature race) on the Saturday and the race itself on Sunday. For those wanting to travel in style, numerous operators offer return helicopter flights to the circuit complete with a champagne breakfast. But be warned, at £500 per person it doesn't come cheap. Once inside, if you haven't got grandstand tickets, the best vantage points can be found at Copse – the first corner on the opening lap provides a spectacular view – Woodcote and Hangar Straight, the fastest part of the track. But wherever you end up, the distinctive aroma of fuel and burning rubber, allied to the deafening cacophony of engines and a partisan home crowd, generates one of the most intense sporting atmospheres on the planet.

▸▸ www.silverstone.co.uk

The 137th Open Golf Championship

WHERE: Royal Birkdale, Lancashire
WHEN: July 17–20, 2008
WHY: The greatest golf tournament in the world returns to one of the greatest ever courses.
WHAT: The Open is back at Royal Birkdale for the first time in ten years and, if this year's championship is half as good as last summer's at Carnoustie, it will be a real thriller. Irishman Padraig Harrington finally ended Europe's eight-year wait for a major championship after a nerve-wracking play-off victory over Sergio Garcia. And, once again, the top players in the world will be in Britain, though all eyes will be on only one man – Tiger Woods. The World No.1 already has three Open Championships to his name and will be looking to follow in the footsteps of fellow American greats Arnold Palmer, Lee Trevino, Johnny Miller, Tom Watson and Mark O'Meara with a triumph at the Lancashire course.

But European golf has never been stronger and there are high hopes the 2008 championship can produce another home winner. Before Harrington's success, Paul Lawrie was the last European to win back in 1999, although his victory was overshadowed by Jean Van de Velde's collapse. The Frenchman needed only a double-bogey down the last to win but lost his nerve, found a stream and eventually made a six to scrape into a play-off, which he lost. Before that, you have to go back to Nick Faldo's 1992 triumph to find a European winner.

However, the Open, the oldest of the four majors, has a history of throwing up unexpected winners and dramatic finishes thanks to the unpredictable British weather. Back in 2004, Ernie Els was cruising to victory when unknown American Todd Hamilton snatched the title in a play-off. Go back nine years and you'll find an even more unlikely winner. "Wild Thing" John Daly put his drink problems behind him to win in the most dramatic fashion possible at St Andrews. The Open consistently delivers drama and excitement and is, quite simply, the one they all want to win.

▸▸ www.opengolf.com

Rip Curl Boardmasters Surf & Music Festival

WHERE: Fistral Beach, Newquay, Cornwall
WHEN: August 4–10 2008
WHY: No need to head to Hawaii or Australia: this is one of the world's greatest beach parties – a week-long fiesta of sun, surfing and sounds.
WHAT: The only world series event in Britain, Boardmasters is part of the global professional surfing circuit and a week-long showcase of the planet's top wave-riders, as well as a two-day music concert on picturesque Fistral Beach. The 2008 line-up is yet to be confirmed but the event attracted some big names last summer with Ash, Paolo Nutini and Guillemots headlining. There are also live sessions every night, with Shikari, Bedouin Sound Clash and Cuban Brothers all appearing last time around.

Fistral also hosts BMX and skateboard exhibitions, where you can watch some of the UK's top stunt riders strut their stuff, bikini contests, beach bars and a trade village selling all the hottest surf wear. While the Boardmasters is, first and foremost, a sporting event, the other attractions which run alongside it give it the feel of a Brazilian carnival – even if the weather isn't always as reliable as at Copacabana.

For those wondering how the UK got to host one of surfing's prestigious and much sought-after world series events, a brief explanation. The sport, according to the British Surfing Association, is a £200 million-a-year industry in the UK. And the British Isles is home to some big waves. Indeed, one spot on the northeastern tip of Scotland is given the accolade of red ink – signifying surfing's black runs – alongside only Hawaii, Tahiti, a remote beach in California and another in Australia. Newquay is also home to one of the world's great waves – the Cribbar, which appears across the bay from Fistral and even has a drink named after it. So, if you're willing to take a chance on the great British weather and keen to cut down on your air miles, head down to Cornwall for one of the summer's biggest and best parties.

▶▶ www.britsurf.co.uk

10 great photography tips for shooting sporting events

1. Most of these events keep spectators well back: you may well need a telephoto lens to take close-up pictures of the action.

2. You will need to use a fast shutter speed to freeze any action. At least 1/500th second, depending on the event.

3. If the light is not good enough for this, you can increase the ISO sensitivity on a digital camera.

4. If you want a simpler way to get a good sports picture, select the sport or action setting.

5. Take pictures of the crowd as well. Their reactions and excitement can be a part of the whole event.

6. Some of the peripheral things, like bars, warm-up areas, pits or even waiting competitors can provide more interesting pictures than the main event.

7. If you can move around, try to shoot from a number of different positions with a range of lenses. It will make your pictures more varied and more interesting.

8. Use the motor-drive or drive mode on your camera if it has one. This will take a number of shots in quick succession making it easier to capture the action.

9. Consider moving the camera in time to the passing subject and shooting with a slow speed. The technique, called panning, will give a blurred background but a sharp subject. It is great for shooting moving cars.

10. Don't forget to photograph the wide shots: a view of the starting grid and stands of the Grand Prix with a wide-angle lens, or a shot showing the entire pitch and clubhouse at Lord's topped with blue sky and clouds can make a great strong shot.

OFFBEAT

Indoor Windsurfing Championships

WHERE: The London Boat Show, Excel, London

WHEN: January 11–20, 2008

WHY: Normally you'd be mad to watch windsurfing in January, but here you can stand in relative comfort watching skills you'd normally only see through a pair of binoculars.

WHAT: Since the London Boat Show moved to Docklands it has become grander in scope, with the docks proving the perfect setting for everything from warships to floating hotels. However, one of the most fun attractions features some of the smallest vessels on show – windsurfers. We've probably all tried windsurfing on holiday at some point, discovering it's not quite as easy as it looks, but embarrassing ourselves only to a few distant watchers onshore. Spare a thought then for the competitors in the Indoor Windsurfing Championships, who have to battle frankly weird conditions a few metres from the eyes of the crowd. A massive indoor tank – providing a 70m course – is whipped up by 24 giant turbines that create a thirty knot wind.

Many of the world's top windsurfers make an appearance here, in competitions that include slalom-style races, freestyle and jump competitions. The slalom races see two boarders race side by side, with full contact often part of the fun. The stunts on display in aerial competition will inspire any budding surfers out onto the water: hanging in the wind on a sail, or somersaulting, are all part of the skills on show. For the jump, the sailors have to line their boards (and, more importantly, their tail fins) up on a ramp. Get it wrong and they face embarrassment and even injury. Get it right, and the results are spectacular.

▶▶ www.londonboatshow.com

Jorvik Viking Festival

WHERE: York

WHEN: February 13–17, 2008

WHY: To keep alive the tradition of Jolablot, the 1000-year-old Viking festival that celebrates the end of the cold dark nights of winter and the coming of spring.

WHAT: Although we usually associate York with the Romans, it was under the rule of the Viking kings until 952AD, when it was known as Jorvik. In 1985, the Viking Festival was started and is now an annual event, attracting thousands of visitors. More importantly, perhaps, it attracts hundreds of Vikings who fight mock battles, engage in longboat races and generally do all things Norse, short of rape and pillage.

Here's where you can see a Viking encampment, watch battle drills, listen to one of the wonderful Norse sagas or go on board a boat. You'll also learn that Vikings didn't have horns or wings on their helmets (they would catch swords and axes) and weren't the barbarians certain English historians have painted them. Er, sorry about the "rape and pillage" allusion above.

When the Vikings conquered York in 866 AD, it was already established as a prosperous city. The invaders built on this history, turning Jorvik into a prime trading post and capital, improving the roads and building an important river crossing. The damp soil preserved much evidence of their life, revealing skilled craftsmen at work, a varied diet and the growing influence of Christianity. The craftsmen were numerous enough to have present-day streets named after them; there's Skeldergate for the shield-makers but, less obviously, Coppergate for carpentry. And there was also a small glass and beadwork industry. The Norsemen played various games, including a board game similar to chess and an early version of backgammon. But, lest all your illusions about Vikings should be shattered, you'll be glad to know that the last king of Jorvik was called Erik Bloodaxe. He killed four of his brothers before being driven out of Northumberland in 954AD. Although Viking York lasted for less than a century, its memory lives on in this Viking Festival.

▶▶ www.jorvik-viking-centre.co.uk

British and World Marbles Championship

WHERE: *Greyhound Public House*, Tinsley Green, West Sussex

WHEN: Good Friday, March 21, 2008

WHY: If you're not excited at the thought of hurling little glass marbles at a hole in the ground, we don't know what's wrong with you.

WHAT: Marbles have been played in Sussex for at least two hundred years and the *Greyhound* has been holding a marbles championship since 1932. Traditionally, the season is from Ash Wednesday to Good Friday, with the last game finishing at noon. Now however, with more than one hundred competitors taking part, the championships go on well into the afternoon.

The format is a knock-out one, with individual and team events. Of course, having a good name for your team is half the battle, gaining you a significant psychological advantage. The International Bright Round Things, Bloody Marbellous or Fast Ferocious Fockers might expect to do well on this score – but clever word play can only take you so far in this ruthless game. Entry is free, as is spectating, but you'll get more out of it if you know a bit about marbles.

You might, for example, think of marbles as a British eccentricity. In 1953, local lad George Burbridge saw an article in a New York paper claiming marbles was "kids stuff". He issued a challenge, saying that if the Yanks could prove it was, we'd give up. Some seven hundred spectators came to watch a venerable local team, which included Arthur "Hydrogen Thumb" Chamberlain, trounce a team of young American sailors 38–11, and a new international rivalry was born. By the 1970s, sponsored US teams were making regular appearances and an American national team was eventually selected from the US Championships to compete. In 1974, the Americans won the event in three straight games, a result that was repeated the following year. The Yanks had arrived, and the rivalry continues unabated today.

▶▶ www.marblemuseum.org

Bodyflight Bedford World Challenge

WHERE: Bodyflight Bedford, Twinwoods Road, Clapham, Bedfordshire

WHEN: March 29–30, 2008

WHY: All the fun of sky-diving, without the endless waiting for packing of parachutes, planes, good weather, or the peering at dots in the sky – what's not to like about the indoor version?

WHAT: Take a skydiving wind tunnel, bring in competitors from all over the world – both professional and amateur – and you have the "most significant international competition for skydivers".

Bodyflight Bedford is the world's largest indoor skydiving wind tunnel, having been converted from a Ministry of Defence aerodynamics test rig by Nottinghamshire businessman Paul Mayer in 2005. The first Bodyflight World Challenge took place there in 2006. Entrants compete for cash prizes and the honour of being the world's best, and all without the hassle of parachutes and planes. The 4-Way teams of – you've guessed it – four have to complete a set routine against the clock while, in the Free Fly event, teams of two perform a mix of set and freestyle moves. In the 4-Way Formation event, divers have only 35 seconds in the tunnel to finish their routine and impress the judges, so high energy is a prerequisite. Free Flyers have a minute in which to show off any new moves.

Sky-diving is generally a solitary sport, but having spectators watching from behind a window adds a whole new dimension. Teams can be mixed male and female and mixed nationality, so a great atmosphere prevails. And, even as the competition has grown from twelve teams in each event in 2006 to thirty in 2007, the whole thing is over in minutes, so no chance for anyone to get bored. In 2007, music was added to the mix and dancing in the air proved a popular innovation. All good practice for busting some moves on the dance floor at the party that rounds off the weekend.

▶▶ www.worldchallenge.info

Medway Sweeps Festival

WHERE: Rochester, Kent

WHEN: Early May, 2008. Final date to be confirmed

WHY: Because if you don't go and see Morris Men in the wild, they might come and dance in your street.

WHAT: It's hard for us now, with Clean Air Acts and central heating, to imagine how central chimney sweeps were to life in the past. It was a hard, dirty life, with small children employed for their ability to climb up into the narrow space above a fire. The sweeps' one day off was May Day when they would parade through Rochester every year, but the outlawing of child labour in the late 1800s saw the event disappear until it was revived in the early 1980s; it has now grown into a three-day event, one of the largest May Day celebrations in the UK.

Central to Medway Sweeps are England's traditional Morris bands who come here from all over the country. Folk groups and other entertainers all add to the atmosphere and there's still a core of sweeps to remind you of the day's origins. With some eighty groups attending last year, this is a chance to learn new dances and songs – activities that carry on into the local pubs every evening. The maypoles start to get their first airings of the year, providing much amusement to spectators if the routines go wrong. Every evening, the marquee on the Castle Green draws the crowds to see some of the UK's finest folk acts perform. If you've wondered what happened to Fairport Convention, here's where you might find out.

Indeed, you might not know much about Morris when you arrive, but you'll be an expert by the time you leave, with traditions from all parts of England on show. "Clogs" and "bobbins" come from the Northern mill towns, while the "handkerchiefs" and "ribbons" are dancers in the Cotswold style. And the ones in leathers, clashing spanners? They're the heavy metal biker Morris Men. The bikers don't make an appearance every year, but several foreign groups are now regular visitors, coming from as far afield as Alaska to join in this very English brand of fun.

▶▶ www.medway.gov.uk/sweepsfestival

Arm Wars XI

WHERE: Trafford Centre, Manchester

WHEN: Usually takes place over the second bank holiday in May

WHY: Where else will you find music blasting out in a pulsating arena, with a host of big burly blokes (and some women) pitting their strength against each other as testosterone levels skyrocket? OK, so maybe at a WWF match, but we know they're less about fight and more about fantasy. To arm wrestle, you have to be hard. Really hard.

WHAT: There was a time when arm wrestling was seen as little more than a legitimized bar-room brawl – over a few pints men would challenge each other for all manner of reasons: to prove how tough they were, to settle a dispute, to win a wager. But over the last decade that's changed, and it's in no small thanks to Neil Pickup, who is to armwrestling what Sly Stallone is to the Rocky film franchise. Pickup's won so many titles with both his arms that his anti-drugs nickname of Natural has been changed to Supernatural. President of the British Armwrestling Federation, he's also overseen the launch of Arm Wars – the UK's premier international armwrestling tournament. In the early days he was organizer, coordinator, commentator and competitor, and he's taken Arm Wars from, pardon the pun, strength to strength over the last decade. What was once seen as a novelty tournament held in small northern backrooms now graces Manchester's Trafford Centre over a weekend in late May, boasting more than ten thousand visitors who watch 150 wrestlers from around the world battle it out for the title in various weights. But what really sets Arm Wars apart from other fight and wrestling gatherings is that the competitors show a distinct lack of airs and graces and will freely mingle with the public.

To top it all, unlike almost every other sport on the planet, this is one where the Brits win more often than not. What more do you want?

▶▶ www.armwrestling.co.uk

Sark Sheep Races

WHERE: Sark, Channel Islands

WHEN: June/July 2008. Final dates to be confirmed

WHY: You'd be foolish to bet on a racing sheep, but surely you can bank on a teddy bear jockey?

WHAT: The tiny island of Sark, the smallest of the four main Channel Islands, sits 80 miles south off the English coast, an hour's boat ride from either Jersey or Guernsey. Famously, it doesn't allow cars, so a bicycle is both the best way to get around and the most appropriate to the pace of the three-square-mile island. But the slowness of life here is forgotten once a year for the annual Sheep Races. All the glamour of Ascot comes to the island, with Pimms, champagne, cucumber sandwiches and strawberries and cream for the elegantly dressed onlookers.

These annual races see sheep, each with a teddy bear jockey mounted on its back, race over a set course, in steeplechase, straight run and open-field events. Once released from the starting gates – and even with the encouragement of a sheep dog – the sheep don't necessarily act in a predictable manner. They tend to huddle together rather than race and are as likely to run away from the finish as towards it. Eventually, however, they make it over the line, causing as much exaltation or disappointment as any race at Royal Ascot. Well, almost.

A professional racing commentator helps us amateurs understand what's going on, while turf accountants and a tote tent will take any money you have no further use for. The Miss Sark Princess (Miss Sark Bo-Peep) competition also reaches its head, while the prizes for the best lady's hat and man's waistcoat bring out old rivalries in the adults. After the excitement of the Saturday races, Sunday is a day for the Carnival Cavalcade, featuring Sark's horse-drawn carriages decorated in their finery, pony rides and other games, such as welly toss and tractor pull. It's time to indulge in some old-fashioned fun and spend your winnings – or console your losses with the thought that all proceeds go to the island's medical fund.

▶▶ www.sark.info

OFFBEAT

World Bog Snorkelling Championship

OFFBEAT

WHERE: Waen Rhydd Bog, Llanwrtyd Wells, Wales

WHEN: August Bank Holiday Monday, August 4, 2008

WHY: When have you ever needed an excuse to wallow in a mud bath? Wearing a rubber suit...

WHAT: Take a 60m muddy trench cut into a peat bog and ask a series of competitors to finish two lengths of it in as short a time as possible, using no conventional swimming strokes, and you have a recipe for fun. Snorkels and flippers are essential, but wet suits are optional – though strongly advised.

Getting tangled in reeds, or just getting completely lost are two of the hazards competitors face. With zero visibility in the bog and the dangers of swallowing a mouthful of bug-infested mud, not to mention the ever-present menace of angering a newt, the race is not quite as simple as it looks. This annual event – dating back to 1985 – claims to attract competitors from all over the world, though the number of Antipodeans working in nearby pubs might boost that statistic. Naturally, the Irish contingent makes a strong showing with the Irish and Northern Irish bog snorkelling champions usually in the running for the title. A woman is the world champion and their times regularly beat those of the men. Joanne Pitchforth's current world record is 1m 35s, with the 2007 champion Rob Liscoe managing "only" 1m 42s.

If bog snorkelling gives you a taste for getting wet and muddy, Waen Rhydd peat bog, near Llanwrtyd Wells, also hosts two other related events on the day. Mountain bike bog snorkelling allows you to ride through the bog on a bike, obviously, while the Bog Snorkelling Triathlon is also just as much fun – or hard work – as it sounds. The bikes are lead-weighted, have tyres filled with water and competitors have to wear diver's weight-belts to keep them down. Anyone can enter – the fee is currently £15 – with all proceeds going to charity.

▶▶ llanwrtyd-wells.powys.org.uk

World Conker Championships

WHERE: Ashton in Northamptonshire
WHEN: 12th October, 2008
WHY: Remember what fun it was when you missed someone's conker and thwacked them on the wrist? Well here you can watch that happen to people all day long.
WHAT: What spectacle better encapsulates British eccentricity than the sight of grown men bashing conkers together in the autumn breeze? And in the quaint Northamptonshire village of Ashton it's not just the men that are at it – the 250 male contestants are joined by around one hundred women each year who then all spend three hours smashing each other's conkers to pieces. The Ashton Conker Club has held the annual World Conker Championships since 1965 when rain stopped play at a cricket match. The soggy cricketers decided they should hold a game of conkers instead, and it proved such a success it's been held ever since.

The contest kicks off at 10.30am, running on eight individual podiums. Strict rules must be adhered to. No nut roasting, vinegaring or other form of tampering is permitted. In fact to guard against underhand practices the club supply all the conkers themselves. They are pre-laced and drawn blind from a bag. Sneaky tactics are also frowned upon. Keeping your conker in one piece by deliberating missing your target, repeatedly "accidentally" getting your string entangled with your opponent's or winding your string to less than 20cm in length will result in a telling-off. Instead just aim squarely at the opposition's conker and give it the best blow you can manage.

Be warned, this Championship isn't spur-of-the-moment stuff either. Those planning to turn up on the day will be disappointed. Players need to register in advance (the deadline in 2007 was October 1) and a £10 registration fee must be paid. Children however can participate in the junior contest without registering. Those lucky enough to emerge triumphant receive a trophy and conker-branded sweatshirt. What more incentive do you need?

▶▶ www.worldconkerchampionships.com

World's Biggest Liar Competition

WHERE: Bridge Inn, Santon Bridge, Holmrook, Cumbria

WHEN: November 2008. Final date to be confirmed

WHY: To see Tom Cruise, Pete Doherty, George W. Bush and, possibly this year, Osama Bin Laden, join a host of international celebrities to pit their wits against one another. Ok, we possibly lied about some of that.

WHAT: Controversy hit the World's Biggest Liar competition in 2003 when 24-year-old kilt-wearing South African Abrie Kruger became the first foreigner to win the title. Local passions were inflamed and he was accused of cheating by telling jokes and reading from a script. That gives you an idea of how seriously they take this event in Cumbria.

The competition has its origins in the late 1800s, when Lake District publican Will Ritson entertained his customers with tall tales of turnips so big that sheep could live inside them. The area is home to Wast Water, England's deepest lake, and Scafell Pike, its highest mountain, so perhaps superlatives came easily to him. Whatever the reason, his legacy is carried on in this annual event, where entrants have to tell tall tales to a panel of judges. They have between two and five minutes to impress. Obviously, no lawyers or politicians are allowed to enter and non-English speaking competitors must provide their own interpreters. No mechanical aids are allowed.

The winner goes away with The Biggest Liar Certificate, and a silk tie emblazoned "The Biggest Liar in the World" as well as the awesome Jennings Trophy. In 2006, comedian Sue Perkins became the first woman champion, with a tale about sheep in the valley creating a hole in the ozone layer after breaking wind, winning out against one entrant who claimed that wind farms are there to propel Britain south to sunnier climes. Perkins gave her £25 prize to a local animal charity. Or so she claimed.

▶▶ www.santonbridgeinn.com

10 great photography tips for shooting offbeat events

1. Try shooting a photo-story. It could convey more about these offbeat events than a single image.

2. Try to make your pictures offbeat as well. Shoot from low viewpoints and try a few funky angles.

3. Offbeat people go for offbeat events. Shoot a range of portraits to show some of the characters; always be polite and courteous when taking pictures of people.

4. Try to place people in context as well as going for head and shoulders portraits.

5. With many of these smaller events you should be able to get closer to the action – giving more engaging and exciting pictures.

6. Consider following a particular participant as they get ready, and then take part in the event. The press office should help you to get in touch with someone in advance.

7. Do your research: you might find some entertaining quirks that will make unique pictures.

8. Shoot close-ups and long shots to give a variety of images.

9. Experiment with slower exposures to introduce movement blur in a few of your pictures.

10. Take a number of shots of each portrait, in case people blink or otherwise look goofy.

CULTURE & FOOD

The Common Ridings

WHERE: Borders, Scotland

WHEN: June & July, 2008

WHY: To celebrate the fact you've seen off the English invaders for another year. Hang on, that can't be right?

WHAT: The Common Ridings of the Scottish Border towns of Hawick, Selkirk, Jedburgh and Lauder are a dawn horseback patrol of the fields that mark each town's boundaries – an event that combines the thrills of Pamplona's Bull Run with the concentrated drinking of Munich's Oktoberfest. The rides are central to life in the Borders: as well as evoking the fierce independence of the region, they display the great sense of camaraderie among Border towns, each of which sends representative riders and a small army of thirsty "Foot Soldiers" to their neighbours' events.

Hawick is the first – and best attended – of the Common Ridings and sets the pattern for the rest. The first evening, Thursday, sees a reception at the town hall during which the town provost hands over the flag to the chief rider, or Cornet, with the words "safe oot, safe in" and the "best lady" ties a ribbon in the town's colours to the flag. If you can't get a ticket, join the huge crowd at The Horse statue on the High Street to watch the Cornet climb up to "buss", or decorate, the statue. Look in also on the Hut on the outskirts of town. After patrolling the town's boundaries on the Thursday and Friday mornings, the Cornet and riders arrive here at 8.30am to settle down for a traditional breakfast of rum and milk, accompanied by rowdy songs and alcohol-soaked male bonding. Tickets are hard to get, but it's worth the effort if you like, er, rowdy male environments.

▶▶ www.hawick.net/common.htm

▶▶ www.hawickcallantsclub.co.uk

Whitstable Oyster Festival

WHERE: Whitstable, Kent

WHEN: Nine days in mid-July, 2008

WHY: Britain produces some of the best oysters in the world, and this is a the perfect opportunity to indulge.

WHAT: An orgy of gluttony that marks the start of oyster season, the festival is an eccentric affair. Starting in the weekend nearest to St James' Day in the last week of July, it runs over nine days, with the opening parade on the first Saturday. The parade, starting with the official Landing of the Catch, follows the progress of the oysters, in a horse-drawn dray, through the town, with stops to deliver the catch to various restaurants, cafés and pubs.

"Fish slappers", women slapping each other over the head with fish, are another feature. Others indulge in the international oyster-opening and eating competition where they devour as many of the delectable bivalves as possible.

But for tourists, it's about enjoying a quaint day by the sea. There are fly-fishing workshops, crab-catching competitions, food fairs and stalls and a brewery festival. For those who like a smidgeon of folk music and an atmospheric pub, the *Old Neptune* is the venue to refresh yourself with a local ale.

Whitstable's oyster celebrations go back a long way. Although it was the Romans who first dredged oysters from the sea on this shingle stretch, the roots of the festival are Norman, when the town was an established fishing port and it was the custom for fishers and dredgers to celebrate with an annual ceremony of thanksgiving. During the major oyster boom in the 1890s, up to one hundred fishing boats were farming sixty million oysters a year. Then the event lost its force. By the 1980s its legacy was dwindling and it was a typical down-at-heel Kent fishing village. Its oysters are famous again today, largely thanks to the entrepreneur Barrie Green, who bought the oyster beds and restored them in the late 1970s. With that resurgence, Whitstable has become a magnet for Londoners who crave a little seaside fun, not to mention an oyster or two.

▶▶ www.whitstableoysterfestival.co.uk

Llangollen International Musical Eisteddfod

WHERE: Llangollen, North Wales

WHEN: July 8–13, 2008

WHY: Forget the coal-black morose reputation that still dogs the Welsh. The Llangollen International Eisteddfod is a joyous, colourful and resoundingly lyrical celebration of music and arts.

WHAT: Started in 1947 as a sticking plaster to heal the scars of the Second World War, the festival has come on in leaps and bounds since emergency ration coupons were used to feed competitors. Back then, a Hungarian choir hitched across France when their trains were cancelled, and a Portuguese ladies choir's first-prize winnings of £50 did little to dent their £1200 travel expenses. But if the financial rewards have been boosted somewhat thanks to some heavyweight sponsors, the essence of the Eisteddfod remains charmingly original. An army of six hundred volunteers runs the event which today attracts fifty thousand visitors, is resolutely non-political and, as the support of its president, Terry Waite, proves – not to mention its 2004 nomination for the Nobel Peace Prize – it is a veritable model of both musical and spiritual harmony.

Not only that – it's trendy too. Ok, there are still the male voice choirs, folk dancers and heaps of children's choirs competing during the daytime. But the new @ SIX performances showcase world music (this year it was rap, reggae, Latin and salsa), and evening concerts are headlined by the likes of Joan Baez, Nashville's Tia McGraff and even tenor José Carreras. Big names to grace the stage over the years have included Shirley Bassey, Michael Ball, Montserrat Caballé and Lesley Garrett, with this year's glittering roll-call kept tightly under wraps until January.

Keep your eyes peeled and you might even spot a superstar of the future. A teenage Pavarotti sang here as part of his father's Modena male voice choir in 1955 (they won, of course), and he returned to perform in 1995. All you have to do now is learn to pronounce the festival title: tongue behind the teeth, now…

▶▶ www.international-eisteddfod.co.uk

Cambridge Folk Festival

WHERE: Cambridge

WHEN: July 31–Aug 3, 2008.

WHY: It's one of the longest running and most famous folk festivals in the world, with a rich heritage of the best established songwriters and new talent, increasingly branching out into all styles of folk, roots and world music.

WHAT: 2008 will be the 44th year of the Cambridge Folk Festival. It began in 1964, when Cambridge City Council approached local firefighter and political activist Ken Woollard, a regular attendee at the newly formed Cambridge Folk Club, and asked him to stage an event. Inspired by a documentary about the 1958 Newport Jazz Festival, Woollard aimed to create an event that preserved the values of the rapidly evolving folk movement, had a friendly family atmosphere and covered a wide spectrum of music, from the UK and Ireland's trad-folk acts, American roots, blues and country artists, old and new singer-songwriters to Bluegrass, gospel, jazz, klezmer and ceilidh.

On the first bill was a young Paul Simon who'd just released *I Am A Rock*, with subsequent early festivals featuring the cream of the folk crop – Joan Baez, John Martyn, The Pogues and Richard Thompson. More recently, artists as diverse as The Proclaimers, Kate Rusby, Amadou & Mariam, Nizlopi and K.T. Tunstall have graced the stage. Many of the artists perform more than once, moving around the three different stages over the course of the weekend.

After scheduled events finish, more music can be found in onsite bars and around campsite fires. Added to all this, there are food and crafts from around the world, music and instrument stalls, a variety of workshops and a designated children's area, The Hub.

Now run by Cambridge City Council following the death of Ken Woollard in 1993, the four-day festival continues to be hugely popular – get booking early. Tickets can be bought either for the whole festival or for individual days, with a ten thousand capacity per day.

▶▶ www.cambridgefolkfestival.co.uk

Brecon Jazz Festival

WHERE: Brecon, Wales

WHEN: August 8–10, 2008

WHY: Mmmm [strokes goatee, plumps beret and smooths down striped boating jacket] jazzzzzzzzz…

WHAT: Ordinary punters and big-name musicians travel from all over the world to come to Brecon, the small Powys market town that sits on the banks of the Usk River with the big, big jazz festival. The three-day festival's Concert Programme sees the greatest names on the scene play to the biggest crowds for the highest prices. Past acts have included some big stars, with everyone from Van Morrison to the fabulous but admittedly less than jazztastic Welsh popsters Super Furry Animals.

Aside from the Concert Programme, there are two other ways to cram in a whole load of other, diverse artists for a fraction of the price, and you can normally get so close that you can see the smoke from the singer's cheroot – or at least you would have been able to before the smoking ban came in.

One option is the Street Music strand – free and open to everyone, with bands assembling throughout the town and on the central bandstand to play to expectant fans. With the exception of 2006, roads through the historic Powys market town are closed to ensure safety, which also greatly enhances the atmosphere. But our favourite option is the fabulous Stroller Programme. Featuring more than fifty acts who perform from Friday through to Sunday, the ticket gives you a wrist band that allows entrance to a host of clubs and venues around the city where names from the English and Welsh scenes appear. This enables you to go on a unique jazz crawl.

The 2007 festival highlighted the work of tenor sax man Joe Lovano, as well as featuring a strand devoted to women in jazz. And 2008 sees the festival's 25th anniversary so it promises to be a big one: details are to be released in May.

▶▶ www.breconjazz.co.uk

Green Man Festival

WHERE: Brecon Beacons National Park, Wales

WHEN: 3 days in mid-August, 2008.

WHY: This small, safe, family-friendly festival has a decidedly left-field folkey bent, consistently strong line-ups and a stunning setting that's tough to match.

WHAT: Created back in 2003 by Jo Bartlett and Danny Hagan of It's Jo And Danny fame, Green Man comes across as a mini-Glastonbury, but without the crowds, crime and chaos. Originally set in the grounds of Craig Y Nos Castle for an event attended by 350 people, the rapidly growing festival now makes its annual home on the Legge-Bourke family's country estate in the heart of the scenic Glanusk valley, surrounded by green hills and with the sparkling River Usk flowing by.

Welcoming, and with plenty of splendid beards on display, Green Man consistently produces great musical line-ups, focusing on folk, with occasional rock, pop and electronica thrown in. The Main Stage is the place to see the better-known names (recent headliners include Bonnie "Prince" Billy, Donovan, Joanna Newsome and Led Zep's Robert Plant), with the FolkeyDokey stage and Green Man Café highlighting new musical discoveries. There are also food stalls, arts and crafts, massage and "spiritual healing" tents, plus film, book events and talks, ranging from Shamanism to Green issues. You can even try your hand at wood carving, knitting or dowsing.

Keeping the festival relatively small means organizers are also able to better manage on-site logistics: plenty of portaloos, showers available, regularly clearing (and recycling) of litter – practical things that make a big difference. The only possible downside is the risk to the spirit of the festival as it gets bigger, though the numbers are set to stay at ten thousand again this year. Even 2007's atrocious weather, turning the ground into a swamp, couldn't dampen the spirits. And when airborne candle lanterns are lit and set floating off into the night sky, high over the silhouette of Sugarloaf Mountain, it's a magical moment. In short, everything you'd hope for from a music fest, and more. Just don't tell anyone else.

▶▶ www.thegreenmanfestival.co.uk

Abergavenny Food Festival

WHERE: Abergavenny, Monmouthshire

WHEN: September 20–21, 2008

WHY: Because this is the Glastonbury of food festivals.

WHAT: It started in 1999 with just thirty stalls, but now thirty thousand hungry visitors pour onto the streets of Abergavenny for a foodie roller-coaster ride. A stellar list of enfant-terrible chefs and portly writers attend: last year saw the hairy wild food TV expert Hugh Fearnley-Whittingstall as well as Mark Hix of *The Ivy*, Giorgio Locatelli, Mitchell Tonks of the chain *FishWorks*, and the *Guardian*'s Matthew Fort. But it's not all tweeds and foodies – the festival is considered a relatively funky affair, with the Arctic Monkeys' label Domino Recordings organizing DJs at the castle for the evening.

Artisan Carmarthanshire cheese, fresh ciders and perries, prestigious Welsh black beef and sumptuous salt marsh lamb (which feeds on natural herbs) are just a few of the delights to sample in the Market Hall, the most hectic area. Expect to fight tough Welsh grannies for the freebies on the food stands. Up at the castle, there is music and a proper dining area for those who aren't full from the free nibbles. You'll also find masterclasses on global foods and can explore new territory for the tastebuds with the Tutored Tastings programmes. Last year, there were chances to revolutionize your tea-drinking habits with Edward Eisler; Mitchell Tonks hosted a "seafood spectacular"; Cyrus Todiwala offered perfect Indian pickles and chutneys; and Elisabeth Luard conducted a hunt for truffles.

But for Martin Orbach, Director of the Festival, it's all about the local food and Welsh characters. Orbach says, "It's the stallholders, the Welsh producers, who are very important. We try to avoid corporate sponsorship, we just provide a showcase for what's going on in Wales." A key tip for foodie-schmoozing is to head to Welsh chef Matt Tebutt's pub the *Fox Hunter*, where celeb chefs gather for drinks when the day's ended.

▸▸ www.abergavennyfoodfestival.com

Open House Weekend

WHERE: All over London

WHEN: Sat 20 & Sun 21 September, 2008

WHY: From residential homes to prison-like corporations, this is your chance to snoop around private architectural splendours.

WHAT: Over six hundred new and old buildings, usually closed to the public, open their doors free of charge for the weekend. It is considered the biggest annual architectural celebration in the UK and was founded as a charity to raise the profile of exceptional buildings. Victoria Thornton, Founding Director of Open House, says: "Experiencing a building in the flesh – inside and out, helps you understand it and assess it, in a way you never could from a picture. If Open House can get Londoners to care passionately about their city and its future buildings, we will really have achieved something."

Twentieth-century modernist classics, ambassadors' residences, private clubs, artists' studios and city banks are just a few of the buildings that open. A popular bastion to see is the Bank of England, built by architect Sir John Soane in the Square Mile. And in Surrey, visitors queue for BedZed, the urban eco-utopia of one hundred homes designed to be carbon neutral and to reduce residents' energy and water usage. In Brixton, locals queue to get inside a windmill dating from 1816 in the heart of the hood, while in the fashionista and design-student's hub Brick Lane in East London, the Huguenot silk merchant's houses of the eighteenth century open their lofty doors – retrace the rich tapestry of migrants who have moved to the area, from persecuted French Huguenots to the Jewish community and more recently Bangladeshi settlers.

Peckham Rye's "15 and a half" Consort Road residential home caused a furore. As seen on Kevin McCloud's TV programme Grand Designs, the opening roof and sliding bath make it an eye-opener. Built on a tight budget on a so-called "unusable" brownfield site, it was shortlisted for the RIBA awards in 2006 and is an inspiration to any wannabe self-builder.

▶▶ www.openhouse.org.uk

Raindance Film Festival

WHERE: London

WHEN: September/October, 2008. Final dates to be confirmed

WHY: As Britain's largest independent film festival, Raindance is a one-stop showcase of the very best and most intriguing indie flicks from the UK and around the world.

WHAT: If mainstream commercial blockbusters don't set your heart racing, head for this two-week long fest to sample the more obscure delights of left-field indie film. The fest is so alternative, in fact, that filmmakers are more likely to roll up by bus than limo, as red-carpet glamour is ditched in favour of quality, progressive movies from low- and no-budget filmmakers. This organic approach is obviously a winning one, as Raindance has built quite a reputation for unearthing the industry's future talent. Responsible for supporting the likes of Shane Meadows who directed *This Is England*, and Christopher Nolan who made *Memento*, it also has a knack for spotting a cult hit in the making, premiering future classics including quirky Johnny Depp vehicle *What's Eating Gilbert Grape?* and Tarantino's *Pulp Fiction*.

At its small-scale inception over fifteen years ago, talent-spotting was fairly easy as a meagre 85 films were submitted and screened, but the festival has grown from strength to strength, and these days thousands of features, shorts and documentaries are vetted before the strongest entries are selected. The final cut is one that established filmmakers and industry sharks tend to keep a key eye on, hoping to back rising young stars. Actors who champion indie movies are also on board, so keep your eyes peeled for a celeb or two at the screenings.

Aside from a potential encounter with a star, the Raindance Film Festival offers the opportunity to catch films that may never make it to your multiplex, from fetish features to politically challenging documentaries. Indeed, there's no better place to keep your finger on the pulse on contemporary film: Raindance should be a must-catch festival on every movie-lover's calendar.

▶▶ www.raindance.co.uk

Belfast Festival At Queen's

WHERE: Belfast, Northern Ireland

WHEN: October/November, 2008. Final dates to be confirmed

WHY: Because the inhabitants of this youthful city know how to party, and there's a wealth of culture on offer too.

WHAT: During Northern Ireland's Troubles, the Belfast Festival kept going, its reputation attracting such stellar names as Moscow State Ballet, the Royal Shakespeare Company and Dexy's Midnight Runners. Also winning a place in Belfast hearts were other, then less well-known performers including Billy Connolly and Rowan Atkinson, who helped cement the festival's reputation as a showcase for new and exciting comic talent.

The event dates back to 1962, and by the 1980s had grown into a two-week celebration of the arts with local performers such as Seamus Heaney, James Galway and Van Morrison headlining events from poetry to music, via theatre, dance, comedy, film and art. With Belfast having undergone a dramatic resurgence, the festival is bigger than ever, now claiming to be the largest arts festival in Ireland and drawing in one hundred thousand visitors. The soaring Waterfront Hall, symbol of the new Belfast, is the main venue, although almost every space in the city hosts something, including the remarkable restored Victorian Grand Opera House.

The year 2007 marked the 45th anniversary, but a funding crisis hit the organizers' ambitious plans, with only a major public outcry, spearheaded by comedian Patrick Kielty, bringing a £150,000 one-off payment from government to guarantee the event. The festival is underway as we go to print, featuring an opening gala concert by The Chieftains and Ulster Orchestra, gigs by The Blind Boys of Alabama and comedy from Sean Lock, Bill Bailey and Sean Hughes. The organizers will need a major rethink for 2008 in order to get their finances back on track, but the event is too central to Belfast's self-image to disappear. If you decide to go along and lend your support, you'll be ensured a great time in the process.

▶▶ www.belfastfestival.com

10 great photography tips for shooting cultural and culinary events

1. Shoot close-ups of food and drink – the macro facility on your camera will make sure you can focus close enough.

2. Try to get hold of a programme of events so that you know what is going on!

3. When shooting people in traditional costume, use a wide aperture to keep the modern-dressed crowds in the background out of focus.

4. For indoor events be careful of colour casts caused by artificial light. The auto white-balance facility should cancel this out if you have a digital camera.

5. Take a tripod to shoot interiors. These will prevent camera shake.

6. To get good pictures of musicians use a telephoto lens to get in close to record the expressions on their faces.

7. In low light, remember that you can boost the sensitivity of a digital camera by selecting a higher ISO.

8. As well as tight portraits, photograph people with a wide lens to show their surroundings.

9. Some of the smaller events at big festivals can be more atmospheric and easier to get close enough to get a good picture.

10. If you are shooting digital, take a lot of pictures. You will have a greater chance of getting quality pictures and you can always edit them later.

ICONIC

Crufts

WHERE: Birmingham NEC

WHEN: March 6–9, 2008

WHY: A four legged friend will never let you down - so imagine the feeling of bonhomie when you're surrounded by 25,000 of the furry blighters. Yes! That's legendary pooch parade Crufts for you!

WHAT: Animal lovers, or merely those in need of a little ray of wet-nosed sunshine in their lives, will thrill at the prospect of this four-day canine jamboree. As well as the dogs themselves, five hundred stalls compete for your attention, touting doggy tiaras, high-end coat conditioner, dog deodorant and even fancy £40-a-time pooper scoopers. Alternatively, beautify your home with a portrait of your pooch or splash out on a dog hydrotherapy pool, yours for just under £30,000.

It's not all spend, spend, spend, though. Those dogs know how to put on a show. Each will have qualified as a champion in some lesser regional contest before they make it to the heady heights of Crufts – the show is named after its founder, Charles Cruft, a dog-biscuit manufacturer who staged his first dog contest in Islington in 1891. Not only are they the epitome of their breed, or genetic freaks depending on your perspective – a dog magazine editor claims the Pekingese have been so in-bred their eyes can fall out at any moment – but they can do tricks. Look on in amazement as they demonstrate their skills in obedience and agility not to mention their dancing skills. Who needs the rollercoaster rides of Alton Towers when you've got the Southern Golden Retrievers Display Team sashaying across the floor like four-footed Ginger Rogerses for entertainment? And that's no shaggy dog story.

▶▶ www.thekennelclub.org.uk

Glyndebourne Festival

WHERE: Glyndebourne, near Lewes, East Sussex

WHEN: May 18–August 31, 2008

WHY: Not only can you soak up the world-class opera, this is a chance to luxuriate in a country house setting while dressing up to the nines.

WHAT: Held since 1934, Glyndebourne Festival Opera was the creation of wealthy landowner John Christie at his 700-year-old family home. Now presided over by his grandson Gus, it's held in an award-winning horseshoe-shaped opera house that opened in 1994. With a vibrant touring schedule, this is a British institution and one also dedicated to education and outreach initiatives. But just because it's out of London, don't expect a cheap night out. It's a popular destination for corporate entertainment and ticket prices for 2007 ranged from £10 (for restricted-view standing) to £185 a seat. There's even a dress code: it's customary to wear black tie or evening dress. Round it off properly with a posh picnic and champers, gen up on your opera facts and be ready to shout "Bravo!" as the curtain comes down.

On the cards for 2008's programme are new productions of Monteverdi's *L'Incoronazione di Poppea*, Humperdinck's *Hänsel und Gretel* (that's Engelbert the German composer, not the perma-tanned crooner) and a new commission – *Love And Other Demons* by Hungarian composer Peter Eötvös, based on Gabriel García Márquez's novel. There are also revivals of previous Glyndebourne productions of Bizet's *Carmen*, Britten's *Albert Herring* and Tchaikovsky's *Eugene Onegin*.

For opera virgins and aficionados, a festival ticket is a real treat. They are hard to come by, but the Glyndebourne experience is one to treasure. Train and coach connections to this little patch of Sussex fit in with performance times. Failing that, you can always land your helicopter in the grounds, with prior permission, of course.

▶▶ www.glyndebourne.com

ICONIC

60 The ROUGH GUIDE to 50 Great UK events

Hay Festival

WHERE: Hay-on-Wye, Powys, Wales

WHEN: May 22–June 1, 2008

WHY: This internationally renowned literary festival was described by former president Bill Clinton as "the Woodstock of the mind."

WHAT: In 1984, Hay festival director Peter Florence and a group of friends sat around his mother's kitchen table and came up with an idea for an event where friends and admired people were invited to "talk, play and hang out." Last year, their creation celebrated its 20th birthday with what has become a characteristically broad and impressive range of international writers, entertainers and thinkers, including Nobel Laureates Orhan Pamuk, Wole Soyinka and Doris Lessing, and musical performers from Baaba Maal to Bryn Terfel.

ICONIC

The friendly little town of Hay-on-Wye, right on the Wales-England border, is known as the second-hand book capital of the world – there are 42 book-shops lining the narrow streets. Having grown from its modest origins, the *Guardian*-sponsored festival is now a twelve-day programme of over 450 events, readings, signings, presentations and talks, covering all kinds of adult and children's fiction, from established authors to hotly tipped new talents, and a range of non-fiction themes, from UK farming and Africa to British democracy, the environment and secularism. There are wine and food stalls too, with lots of sampling opportunities.

Having established sister festivals in Italy, Brazil, Colombia and Spain, Hay is set to launch in the US and in Africa in 2008. It's the original Hay, though, where you're likely to rub shoulders with some of the many writers who've sung the festival's praises. Event prices range from free to around £35, with many of the big-name readings and talks selling out fast. Early booking is also advised for accommodation; you might want to bag a pitch in the town's temporary campsite.

▶▶ www.hayfestival.com

Henley Royal Regatta

WHERE: Henley-on-Thames, Oxfordshire

WHEN: July 2–6, 2008

WHY: Do you really need an excuse to spend a day on the booze by one of the most beautiful spots on the Thames in the height of summer? Thought not.

WHAT: What-ho old chap. It's time to slip on some chinos and boating shoes, don the old school tie and striped blazer and dust off the straw boater. We're off to Henley to mess around on the Thames while we get blotto on Pimms, gin and tonic and champers.

The Henley Royal Regatta is without doubt one of the social events of the year and, if Lord's is the spiritual home of cricket, then Henley is the playground of Jeeves and Wooster. For Henley is an event, to coin an old phrase, that is as old as the hills and twice as dusty. The first festival here was set up by the town's mayor way back in 1839 as a fair with other amusements, but it wasn't long before amateur rowing took over. The only years the Regatta has not been held since was during both the First and Second World Wars. The more serious business – featuring many Olympic hopefuls – includes some hundred races per day with starts coming every five minutes and nineteen events in total: six for Eights, five for Fours (3 coxless and 2 coxed), four for quadruple sculls, and races for coxless pairs and double sculls. There are also single sculling races for both men and women.

There are two main reasons for coming here as a mere mortal: you're on a corporate jolly in one of the many pavilions by the river and you're caning the free booze, or you enjoy a darn good laugh sitting in a bankside pub chuckling at the rocketing levels of inebriation. For make no mistake, alcohol plays a large part in the Regatta. Why more people don't end up in this, thankfully, rather calm section of the Thames is a mystery.

▶▶ www.hrr.co.uk

The Artois Championships

WHERE: Queen's Club, West Kensington, London

WHEN: June 9–15, 2008

WHY: As the prequel to Wimbledon, the enticing grass courts at Queen's attract most of the world's best male players.

WHAT: Founded in 1886 – and named after Queen Victoria, its first patron – Queen's Club was the world's first multipurpose sports complex. Now, with 28 courts – which four-time winner Andy Roddick has called "arguably the best in the world" – it is the venue for the annual Queen's Club Championships, one of the top-ten global tennis championships. With the clay court French Open only a few weeks beforehand and Wimbledon following shortly afterwards, this is a chance for the top players – both singles and doubles – to brush up their grass-court techniques. It's a vital event in the professional calendar, where grass is otherwise seldom experienced. There's also big prize money at stake, second only to Wimbledon itself, and the winners here are usually good pointers to the results on grass for the rest of the year. In 1985, a relative unknown called Boris Becker lifted the trophy, before becoming the youngest-ever Wimbledon champion.

Queen's retains a unique atmosphere of its own, an oasis of tennis in the middle of red-brick London back streets. Walk out of Barons Court tube, through the inconspicuous club gates, and the courts slowly reveal themselves – packed into a tiny area. The surroundings are certainly cramped for visitors – and the queues for strawberries and cream seemingly endless – but the lovely courts themselves do justice to the skills on show… As the sun comes down over the beautifully manicured centre court, with that unique light you get only on an English summer evening, you'll understand what impresses Andy Roddick so much.

▸▸ www.queensclub.co.uk

ICONIC

Royal Ascot

WHERE: Ascot, Berkshire

WHEN: June 17–21, 2008

WHY: To see and be seen. To wear your biggest, best and most eye-catchingly outrageous hat, or a smart topper for the gents. To eyeball the Royals and to try and muscle your way into the Royal Enclosure. Oh, and to watch the odd horse race.

WHAT: This prestigious event in the English social calendar has a history dating back to 1711 and is attended by around 300,000 people over the course of its five days. The most important guests are, of course, the royal family, and their arrival each day in a horse-drawn carriage is an essential part of the event's mystique. In 2008, prize money of £4m will be won, attracting the world's best horses and jockeys. The highlight of the event is the Ascot Gold Cup, held on the Thursday, known as Ladies' Day. Dating back to 1807, the Gold Cup is a flat race run over 2 miles, 4 furlongs, which jockey Lester Piggott won an incredible eleven times. This year the Gold Cup will have a prize of £250,000, but no race is now worth less than £60,000.

Many of the visitors, however, have no interest in racing at all and competition can be fierce to gain admittance to the Royal Enclosure. Here, a strict dress code applies, with men in morning dress – tails and top hats, with grey being a popular colour for Ladies 'Day – while women must wear hats. Flamboyant hats have become a major part of Ladies' Day for both the women who wear them and the media, who focus on the most outrageous and expensive ones.

However, even if you're not in the Royal Enclosure you can still enjoy dressing up for the day. And out on the rails, whether you're a seasoned gambler or a nervous first-timer, the excitement and the atmosphere are the same. And the champagne tastes just as good.

▶▶ www.ascot.co.uk

Hampton Court Palace Flower Show

WHERE: Hampton Court Palace, East Molesey, Surrey

WHEN: July 8–13, 2008

WHY: Quite simply, it's the largest flower show in the world and boasts the most stunning historical backdrop imaginable.

WHAT: The Royal Horticultural Society hosts three main flower festivals over the course of the summer season: Chelsea, Hampton Court Palace and Tatton. While Chelsea may be the media darling, with crowds of celebs attending and a chi-chi location, it's actually quite a small show, whereas Hampton Court is huge. The fact that it's in such a glorious historical setting and falls smack bang in the middle of the summer just adds to its allure.

Over the six days of the show, garden-obsessed guests can visit more than fifty wonderful display gardens including the "tranquil" and "children's" displays, as well as more outré conceptual gardens created by budding designers. Meanwhile, the various abundant flower marquees and the Festival of Roses have displays by hundreds of the UK's top nurseries. And, if you fancy yourself as a tad green-fingered there are also a host of gardening accessories, seeds and a vast range of other kit on sale to help make your garden blossom.

Hampton Court's history includes some of the greatest names of sixteenth-century Britain. Henry VIII, Christopher Wren and Thomas Wolsey all had a hand in creating one of the finest royal palaces in the country – that the magnificent house is overshadowed during the show is ample proof of what a visually spectacular event this is. Oh, and Britain being a nation of gardeners, naturally this is a popular one. Tickets go on sale as early as November, so book early to avoid missing out.

▶▶ www.rhs.org.uk

Skandia Cowes Week

WHERE: Cowes, Isle of Wight

WHEN: August 2–9, 2008

WHY: Because it's not about the sailing. Although, if you like sailing, it's about that.

WHAT: Put on your stripy pullover, pull on your sailing shoes and head down to the Isle of Wight for Cowes Week. If you can carry off a jaunty skipper's cap, so much the better.

Of course, you might be one of the unlucky ones who has to put to sea, whatever the weather, and actually race in a yacht. If so, we look forward to seeing you in the bar after the race when you can regale us with stories about losing your spinnaker in a squall. We'll be in one of the countless hospitality marquees, sampling the product of whatever drinks company is keeping us out of the sun or rain (Champagne Mumm or Pimms for preference), whilst chatting up the pretty people who descend on Cowes for this annual event.

Dating back some 170 years, Cowes Week has grown from a party in a few boat sheds to a fully-fledged music, food and drink festival. The new £1.3m Haven Events Centre provides state-of-the-art facilities as the South Coast's biggest bands blast away through the PA.

Yachtsmen – from amateurs to Olympic and World champions – come from all over the world to compete at Cowes. Some thousand yachts and eight thousand sailors will be racing for honour and prizes (on a date traditionally – and somewhat obscurely – fixed around the first Saturday after the last Tuesday in July).

However, even those with little interest in sailing itself will enjoy the beauty of a lovely sunset, watching boat after boat swoop home after a hard day's racing. In the evening, the hard-working crews party hard with a series of balls, and the week climaxes with an impressive fireworks display on the final, prize-giving Friday.

▸▸ www.skandiacowesweek.co.uk

Edinburgh Festival

WHERE: Why, Edinburgh, of course.

WHEN: Late summer, with 2008's Edinburgh International Festival running from August 8–31.

WHY: There's something for everyone as the Scottish capital's festivals deliver the best of theatre, music, film, dance, circus and every other performing art under the sun.

WHAT: Summer in Edinburgh is festival season. At the centre of it all is the Edinburgh International Festival, which started in 1947 to provide "a platform for the flowering of the human spirit" and to help heal the wounds of the Second World War. Since then, several other jamborees have been established alongside, including the International Film Festival, the Fringe, the Jazz Festival, the Book Festival, the Mela and the Art Festival – collectively known as the Edinburgh Festival(s).

The International Festival features a programme of classical music, opera, theatre and ballet at seven key venues: the Usher Hall, Festival Theatre, Edinburgh Playhouse, King's Theatre, the Royal Lyceum Theatre, Queen's Hall and The Hub. But the Fringe is arguably now the most vital component in the mix. Featuring theatre, comedy, music, dance, circus and other performance arts, it's a chance to see the good, the bad and the bizarre, from professional theatre companies to drama students blowing their loans on their own productions. At the height of festival fever, Edinburgh's Royal Mile is packed with an energized mass of tourists, jugglers, buskers and performers plugging their shows, while every room or cupboard that can possibly cram in more than three people is turned into a performance space. Tickets can be pricey, but there are bargains and even freebies to be found. Some less established companies hand out tickets to ensure they have an audience to perform in front of – it's often worth a gamble and part of the fun of the Fringe.

▶▶ www.edinburghfestivals.co.uk
▶▶ www.eif.co.uk ▶▶ www.edfringe.com

ICONIC

Braemar Highland Gathering

WHERE: Braemar, Aberdeenshire, Scotland

WHEN: September 6, 2008

WHY: To see big men in kilts – why else?

WHAT: If you're the kind of person who associates Scotland with tartan, kilts and sporrans then you've come to the right place – the Braemar Highland Gathering is the daddy of all highland games. If past events are anything to go by, you'll be entertained before a single caber has been tossed. In 2003 the 18,000-strong crowd booed and swore at then Prime Minister Tony Blair, while a 12-year-old flower girl presenting a posy to the Queen described him as a "nasty man". To top that off, the games' official starter, a 75-year-old man from Fife, accidentally shot himself in the hand with his starting pistol. Oops.

Ok, so there aren't many real Highlanders left in the Highlands but you'll still be treated to quite a spectacle when you arrive in the quaint Aberdeenshire village. Dancers, bands and pipers perform alongside each other while braw laddies toss the caber, putt the stone and throw the hammer. It's not all strength events – other popular games include the relay race, hill race, long leap and the children's sack race. Anyone can take part, and you'll find children mixing with international athletes. This year teams from H.M. Forces will compete in relay races and a tug-of-war championship.

There's been a gathering of some sort for the past nine hundred years and the Queen, who is patron of the gathering, attends most years. Queen Victoria, famously a great fan of Scotland's stunning scenery, was the first patron of the games. A final word: it's as cold as it is beautiful up here in Braemar, so be sure to wrap up warm.

▶▶ www.braemargathering.org

10 great photography tips for shooting iconic events

1. The most difficult thing at big, organized events is to get close enough to take pictures. If you can't do this, a telephoto lens can help you to get close-up shots.

2. If you can't get in close enough, consider taking pictures of the reactions of the crowds.

3. Try to find a high viewpoint to shoot above the crowds.

4. Avoid shooting into the light if you can, as this will cast your subject into shadow.

5. Ascot is famous for the hats on Ladies' Day – try taking a range of portraits of ladies in hats. You'll need to be at your most charming and courteous for this!

6. When photographing people in hats, you might need to use fill-in flash to avoid deep shadows on their faces: this can even be done on a compact camera using the "forced flash" setting.

7. The flower show is perfect for taking beautiful close-ups of exotic flowers. Use the macro setting on your camera or lens to make sure the flower isn't too close to be in focus.

8. Many of the events are famous for being on the social calendar. Try photographing high society at play.

9. At the races, place yourself at the start or finish line to get the most exciting shots.

10. At the Edinburgh Festival don't forget the Fringe: you can get some great portraits of street entertainers.

ICONIC

SPECTACLE

Aviemore Sled Dog Rally

WHERE: Loch Morlich, Aviemore, Scotland
WHEN: January 19 & 20, 2008
WHY: To see around two hundred teams of dogs and their mushers (owners) race each other in the shadows of the Cairngorms.
WHAT: You'd normally expect to go off to the icy depths of Alaska or Greenland to see husky dogs pulling a sledge, but Scotland has been home to this event since the 1980s. Bizarrely, we have *Blue Peter* to thank for planting the seeds, when the show's Peter Duncan came up to Aviemore to train for a race in Alaska. Twenty mushers entered the first race – with only twelve showing up on the day, due to bad weather.

Nowadays, up to two hundred mushers, ranging from eight years old – there are around forty juniors – to sixty-year-olds, race their teams of between two and eight dogs at around 30mph along the 7km rough track.

The trail itself is a rough cross-country ski course through Aviemore's forests. Of course, snow isn't reliable in the UK, but the race goes ahead anyway with dogs pulling three-wheeled rigs. While not as picturesque as a snowy landscape, the forest floor makes the skills of the musher even more crucial. One surprising entrant in 2006 may have appreciated the warmer conditions. Jamaican Devon Anderson, who had never seen snow, took part in the 2006 event, finishing an impressive 27th out of forty competitors. Amazingly, he trained with a team of mongrels rescued from Kingston's dog pound.

Around the main race, where you'll see more than one thousand dogs – Siberian huskies, Alaska Malamutes, Samoyeds, Greenland Dogs and Canadian Eskimo breeds – there are a range of additional activities, the most popular being the Trek. Although not a race, it isn't for the inexperienced musher and dogs, but does allows potential race entrants to increase their skills by running in groups.

▶▶ www.siberianhuskyclub.com

Up Helly Aa

WHERE: Lerwick, Shetland

WHEN: The last Tuesday of January, falling on January 29 in 2008

WHY: For 24 hours of festivities, with a burning galley, costumes, dancing and lots of booze.

WHAT: Shetland's Up Helly Aa Viking Fire Festival proves the theory that islanders know how to party. Themed around Shetland's Viking past, it starts with a procession through the town of "Guizer squads" – local men wearing handmade Viking costumes, carrying shields and axes – led by the Viking chief or "Guizer Jarl". After proudly displaying a specially made life-size Viking ship, they march to the town square to make their annual proclamation, mocking local officials. In the afternoon, the Fiery Sessions concert at the Garrison Theatre is a must-see for music fans, featuring family ensembles, renowned soloists and energetic young bands.

Everything kicks off at night with more than a thousand men, in costumes ranging from Vikings to vampires to strippers, and each carrying a burning paraffin torch, make their way around the town, giving the night sky a smoky orange glow. The Guizers make a giant circle around the dragon-headed Viking ship, chant, sing, and then throw their torches onto the galley, setting it alight. After the flames die down, it's off into the night for parties at halls and pubs around the town, featuring traditional music and dancing. Until the early hours of the morning, Guizer squads tour from hall to hall, each performing a specially created dance, comedy or theatre routine – often shambolic, as you'd expect after a day's drinking. Festivities carry on long into the next day, when sorry-looking stragglers, still in costume, can be seen wandering the streets.

While much of the festival is open to the public, hall events are meant primarily for locals. Tickets for tourists can be hard to come by, so it's worth putting your name down at various hotels or contacting the tourist information office well in advance.

▶▶ www.visitshetland.com/events/up-helly-aa-event

Chinese New Year

WHERE: Strand, Trafalgar Square and Soho, London
WHEN: February 10, 2008
WHY: A pageant of colour, dance and noise, these celebrations show off the best of Chinese culture. It's just one of the many facets of London – home to the largest Chinese community in Europe – that make it one of the world's great cities.

WHAT: Since their inception in 1973, the Chinese New Year celebrations around London's Chinatown have grown to such an extent they now regularly attract crowds of more than half a million. The day starts at 11am with a colourful parade along the Strand and down Shaftesbury Avenue. From noon, a stage in Trafalgar Square is the centre of events, with dragon and lion dances and artistes from the UK and China entertaining the crowd with both modern and traditional music and arts. Always popular are the Shaolin Monks, showing off their martial arts skills. Meanwhile, Leicester Square throbs with stalls offering everything from food to fashion, books to massage and, of course, fortune-telling for the year ahead.

If you want to see the parade, featuring dancers, acrobats and papier-mâché lions devouring cabbages hung from the upper floors, try to position yourself under one of the cabbages and stand your ground. The noise is deafening, with drums banging and fire-crackers going off incessantly, and many of the crowd bringing whatever they can lay their hands on or buy – such as Chinese hand-drums – to add to the cacophony. Of course, the Chinese invented fireworks and they are an essential part of the celebrations, with shows at 2pm and 5pm.

As the evening draws in, the crowds move toward Chinatown itself, centring on Gerrard Street with its Oriental Gates and pagoda-style telephone boxes. Street performers and dancers vie with each other for the best spot to entertain while diners cram the many restaurants and cafés. It's the Year of the Rat in 2008, an animal considered by the Chinese to be courageous and enterprising.

▸▸ www.chinatownchinese.com

SPECTACLE

Royal Show at Stoneleigh

WHERE: Stoneleigh Park, Kenilworth, Warwickshire

WHEN: July 3–6, 2008

WHY: The Royal Show will get you back in touch with your country roots – and up close and personal with a combine harvester.

WHAT: The Royal Show is all about experiencing the countryside without having to get your boots too dirty or, for that matter, having to listen to *The Archers*. If you've a passion for countryside and livestock, or any interest at all in the business and technological innovations in the farming industry, the show will bring you bang up to speed. Or, of course, you can just go along for some good food, cider or beer, and a great day out – this kind of outing is always a winner with kids.

A perennial favourite with the grown-ups though is the Food Pavilion, dedicated to showcasing some of the finest speciality producers of regional food and drink, from cheese and wine to hams, bacon and honey. If you've an eye for a pig, goat, cow or even an alpaca, over 6500 animals are on show demonstrating the best of breeding excellence, with awards given for Supreme Male and Female of each breed. And if it's the latest developments in tractor engines that get your pulse racing, the Machinery Awards and estate maintenance area will appeal.

The show also runs free conferences in the Rural Business Centre, an opportunity to get to grips with key and contentious industry issues. High-profile speakers examine animal health, food trace ability, environment and global markets. After the hammer-blows that have hit the British countryside in recent years – from foot-and-mouth to the bluetongue outbreak – and the growing popularity of organic food, these debates bring a serious side to all the fun. Lifestyle – of the rural kind that is – isn't neglected either, with various aspects of British country life on show in the Country Lifestyle area that houses specialist exhibits as well as the action-packed Countryside Arena and the popular Flower Show.

▶▶ www.royalshow.org.uk

Great Yorkshire Show

SPECTACLE

WHERE: Great Yorkshire Showground, Harrogate

WHEN: July 8-10, 2008

WHY: If tha dunt go t't Gret Yorkshire Sho, tha dunt know tha a born. Ya daft apeth.

WHAT: They say "there's nowt so queer as folk" and the Great Yorkshire Show illustrates the point fabulously. For while Tykes get famously stereotyped for everything from having deep pockets with short arms to a belligerent, arrogant attitude, no one seems to give them credit for hosting one of the greatest, most gobsmackingly amazing agricultural shows in the whole country.

Back in the 1830s, a group of Yorkshire farmers got together and decided to set up a county-wide agricultural society that could both provide a common front on common issues and help organize an annual show of its members' wares. The first show took place in 1834, and was attended by a few thousand people in flat caps. Little could those founding members of the Yorkshire Agricultural Society have expected that 150 shows later (the anniversary is in 2008), the event would be attended by more than 150,000 people – still in flat caps. But head up to the spa town of Harrogate, where a special showground has been in operation since the 1950s, and it's easy to see why the GYS, as it's known, has become the biggest agricultural-related event in the north of England.

Around the 250 acres of the show you can lose yourself amidst (and take a deep breath before you read this) dancing diggers; livestock including cattle, sheep, horses, goats, pigs and rabbits; working blacksmiths shoeing horses; fly-fishing demos; sheep-shearing and sheep-dog displays; honey gathering; fashion shows; sheep races; market stalls selling all manner of goods; show jumping with a host of top professionals; army bands; stickmaking, woodcarving and woodturning… And that's all before breakfast. We can't even begin to list in the space we have all the events that unfold over the following 72 hours.

▸▸ www.greatyorkshireshow.com

Royal International Air Tattoo

WHERE: RAF Fairford, north of Swindon, Gloucestershire

WHEN: July 12–13, 2008

WHY: If you only go to one airshow in your life, make it the biggest and the best in the world.

WHAT: One minute you are rooted to the spot by the earth-trembling roar of a Tornado fighter jet making a fast and low pass, the next you are marvelling at the surprising agility of the giant Boeing 747 jumbo jet as its pilot throws it around the sky. Almost immediately, you can be left momentarily blinded by coloured smoke from the jet trainers of the Italian Frecce Tricolori display team.

Welcome to RAF Fairford on the edge of the Cotswolds, where every year for one mad and (usually) gloriously hot summer weekend, more than 150,000 people gather for THE event on the world's airshow calendar. What attracts families and anoraks alike is a gathering of more than three hundred aircraft. In 2007 the highlights of the eight-hour daily flying display included a rare appearance outside their own country by the United States Air Force's Thunderbirds, with their Top Gun-style showmanship throwing down a challenge for our own Red Arrows to match. It's also a chance for the British public to see where their taxes are being spent, with set-piece demonstrations showing what RAF aircraft including the new £125million (yes, each) Typhoon fighter can do.

But the real essence of the show, and something that has carried on from the first event held in 1971, is the coming together of pilots from all over the world, often from air forces on opposing sides back home. Down the years Israelis have parked next to Jordanians, Turks next to Greeks and Russians next to Americans. Pakistan visited for the first time last year, India this year. The pilots hang out by their planes all day and are always happy to chat to the public.

▸▸ www.airtattoo.com

Discovery Channel International Balloon Fiesta

WHERE: Ashton Court Estate, Bristol

WHEN: August 7–10, 2008

WHY: To see an eye-popping 150 hot air balloons taking to the sky in a tranquil tableau of shapes and colour.

WHAT: The balloon fiesta has been running for 28 years and is the largest event of its kind in Europe, giving spectators who opt to take a ride a bird's-eye view of the beautiful Ashton Court Mansion and its surrounding estate. Every morning and evening (weather conditions permitting) there's a glorious mass ascent of balloons. If you've ever wanted to take to the skies, now is your chance – hop into the basket with video cam or camera at the ready and capture the experience.

The balloons gathered from all over the world include some weird and wonderful designs such as the Piper, The Monster and the Shopping Trolley. Hot-air balloon enthusiasts are on hand to chat, swap tips, tell you all about taking to the skies and introduce you to the experience. If you prefer to stay on the ground there's plenty to keep land lovers interested from early morning, with shows and displays, jousting, funfairs and field-gun demonstrations. And after lunch a line-up of pop stars take to the stage for some live music. When night falls it's time for the nightglow spectacle when around thirty tethered balloons make their ascent, illuminating the sky with a choreographed sequence set to music. A firework display finishes this *son et lumière* with a difference.

All the balloon activities are dependent on the weather, but you'll be able to see tethered balloons every day. In recent years, the fiesta has also introduced "Heaven" – a relaxed interactive zone with seating and a separate small stage for music and entertainment away from the hustle and bustle of the main arena. The atmosphere is described as a "festival within a festival", offering an oasis of calm and tranquillity that will also stretch the imagination and entertain throughout the day.

▶▶ www.bristolfiesta.co.uk

England's Medieval Festival

WHERE: Herstmonceux Castle, East Sussex

WHEN: August 23–25, 2008

WHY: To experience the thrills, spills, sights, sounds – but thankfully not smells – of merrie medieval England.

WHAT: Fifteenth-century moated Herstmonceux Castle provides a historic backdrop to this festival that lovingly recreates a medieval village and various key events that bring the era to life. The most dramatic is when a thousand knights, bowmen and men-at-arms lay siege to the castle during the day. Squads of archers fire off storms of arrows, along with cannon fire and various other ancient weapons.

The longbow tournament draws some of the finest bowmen in modern Europe. Admire their skills and then have a go yourself – they're happy to pass on tips. Otherwise take the minstrel-like option and just stroll around, taking in merchants and craftsmen displaying their skills on Medieval Traders Row, or drop into a medieval tavern for a plate of roast hog and some traditional ale. Tankard in hand, you can take in the parades which feature a dancing bear (yes, it's a man in a suit), tumblers, fire-eaters and horse-riders portraying the many pilgrims from Chaucer's *Canterbury Tales*. You can also watch falconry displays, listen to strolling minstrels, cheer the puppeteers, browse or buy at the craft stalls, or learn a bit more about the Middle Ages at the living history encampments.

And, of course, the jousting area features the dangerous games of skill that were so much a part of a knight and squire's essential training. These include "Running the Ring" (collecting suspended rings with a 7ft lance), "Course of Heads" (riding at a course of cabbages set on posts) and "Melee" (a contest of skirmish between two teams). Difficult tricks on horseback, even without wearing heavy plate armour. Finally, be warned: many of those taking part this year probably came in previous years as a bit of a laugh. And buying your own armour is never cheap.

▸▸ www.renaissancefestival.com

Bristol International Festival of Kites & Air Creations

WHERE: Ashton Court Estate, Bristol

WHEN: August 30–31, 2008

WHY: Have you ever walked past a group of people in a park flying kites and not craned your neck to the sky? Exactly.

WHAT: Believe it or not, there is such a thing as a kite nerd. Martin Lester, John Peyton and Avril Baker were three of them back in the mid-80s when they came up with the idea of the Bristol Kite Festival. And armed with a budget of £300 they marched into the local council and asked to launch an event. Their request was granted and, despite the untimely death of Peyton before the first festival, Bristol has grown to be one of the world's premier kiting events, drawing other kite nerds from all over the globe.

Unlike other nerds, such as those with an unhealthy fascination for *Star Trek* or *Buffy The Vampire Slayer*, kite nerds actually make us happy as they do such cool stuff. Not only do they achieve that ancient desire of man and get things to fly, but when they do they use daring shapes and structures to paint the sky with myriad colours. Lastly, they do it for love and their and our entertainment – there are no lucrative sponsorship deals in kiting.

So what does one see every summer in Bristol? Well over two days there are all sorts of displays: synchronized and choreographed, educational (take a look at the tips given for flying Asian fighting kites – truly astounding), sports kites, mass flying and aerobatics. There are also radical sports such as kitesurfing and buggying that increase the drama levels. You'll see teams here from all over the world, while in 2007 inflatables were added to the lineup, just in case there wasn't enough for us to see. Some of the teams even display a sense of humour, with names such as Pulling Power. Did we mention we love kite nerds?

▶▶ www.kite-festival.org

SPECTACLE

Lewes Bonfire Night

WHERE: Lewes, East Sussex

WHEN: November 5, 2008

WHY: All the stuff you're not allowed to do as a kid is encouraged here – you can play with matches, let off fireworks, drink, burn effigies…

WHAT: "Throughout recorded history, it has taken very little persuasion to get English people to make a bonfire." So said *The Oxford Dictionary of English Folklore*, and as burnt-out cars on estates across the land testify, our fire-starting tendencies are still going strong. How better to spend a cold November night than by indulging in some passive arson at the nation's biggest and best bonfire night?

Venice may have its masked Carnival and Siena its medieval horse race, but the small Sussex town of Lewes punches above its weight with a festivity featuring costume, heraldic-style gangs and naked flames that have left many a bearded man slightly singed. Six Bonfire Societies, representing different areas of the town, each take part in a procession along the high street before staging their own flame-thrilled events. Set up in the mid-1800s to suppress the sometimes over-eager activities of anarchic rioters known as the Bonfire Boys, the Societies acknowledge their predecessors (who disguised themselves as smugglers) with Where's Wally-style "smuggler colours" of striped jumpers and knitted caps. There are also two different types of costume for members, ranging from Vikings, Moors and Zulu warriors to Tudor ladies and Siamese dancers.

Alongside bands, banners and flaming torches, blazing tar barrels are dragged through the streets, marchers drop bangers and miniature firework displays based on topical themes, or tableaux, are lit while being carried. Effigies of heroes and "enemies of the bonfire" – often identifiable characters with a Catholic bent, such as Guy Fawkes or Popes from times of religious persecution – are paraded to the Societies' bonfires. These generally require a ticket, so it's advisable to book in advance.

▶▶ www.lewesbonfirecouncil.org.uk

10 great photography tips for shooting spectacular events

1. Try to find out as much as possible about what is happening in advance, so that you will know what to go and where to shoot.

2. Big events are all about mobility: don't take so much kit that you can't move around easily.

3. Take a range of lenses, or a zoom lens, so you will be able to shoot close-ups and wide shots.

4. Don't spend the whole time chasing the action. Find a good spot, and let the action come to you.

5. Use a telephoto lens to isolate people and things from the crowd surrounding them.

6. Shoot from a low angle with a wide-angle lens to give a dynamic exaggerated perspective.

7. Make like a boy scout and be prepared: you will miss shots if your camera is left in a bag on your back.

8. For Lerwick and Lewes, use a high ISO and a manual exposure, metering just away from the fires so you can take pictures of people illuminated by the flames.

9. If you do use fill-in flash for these events, fit a warm-up filter on the lens – so it will balance the firelight, otherwise it will come out too blue in comparison.

10. For fast-moving events, use autofocus and auto-exposure to let your camera do some of the work for you.

ROUGH GUIDES

Britain

iPhone

Edinburgh DIRECTIONS

His Dark Materials

Devon & Cornwall

Wales

Paris

Make the most of
your time on Earth™

Events by Month